THE ROYAL COURT
THEATRE PRESENTS

Escaped Alone

by Caryl Churchill

Escaped Alone was first performed at the Royal Court Jerwood Theatre Downstairs, Sloane Square, on Thursday 21 January 2016.

Escaped Alone

by Caryl Churchill

CAST (in alphabetical order)

Mrs Jarrett **Linda Bassett**
Sally **Deborah Findlay**
Lena **Kika Markham**
Vi **June Watson**

Director **James Macdonald**
Designer **Miriam Buether**
Lighting Designer **Peter Mumford**
Sound Designer **Christopher Shutt**
Associate Director **Stella Powell-Jones**
Assistant Director **Roy Alexander Weise**
Casting Director **Amy Ball**
Production Manager **Tariq Rifaat**
Costume Supervisor **Lucy Walshaw**
Stage Manager **Dan Gammon**
Deputy Stage Manager **Sophie Rubenstein**
Set Built by **Miraculous Engineering**
Scenic Work by **Kerry Jarrett**
Cyclorama by **Gerriets Great Britain Ltd**
Specialist Lighting Effects by **Howard Eaton Lighting Ltd**
Draughting by **Emma Pile, Paul Halter**
Production Electrician (Tour) **Marec Joyce**
Production Sound Engineer (Tour) **Sean Ephgrave**
Transport **Southern Van Lines**
Shipping **Sound Moves**

The Royal Court & Stage Management wish to thank the following for their help with this production:
Wildflower Turf Ltd, Regent's Park Open Air Theatre, Hannah Falvey.

Production supported by Anatol Orient in memory of Ruth Bloomfield.

Escaped Alone
by Caryl Churchill

Caryl Churchill (Writer)

Plays include: **Owners, Traps, Light Shining in Buckinghamshire, Cloud 9, Top Girls, Fen, Serious Money, Ice Cream, Mad Forest, The Skriker, Blue Heart, This is a Chair, Far Away, A Number, Drunk Enough To Say I Love You?, Seven Jewish Children, Love & Information, Here We Go, and Pigs & Dogs.**

Linda Bassett (Mrs Jarrett)

For the Royal Court: **Escaped Alone, Love & Information, In Basildon, Wastwater, The Stone, Lucky Dog, Far Away, The Recruiting Officer, Our Country's Good (& West End), Serious Money (& West End/Public Theatre, NY), East is East (& Tamasha/Birmingham Rep/Theatre Royal Stratford East/West End/UK tour); Aunt Dan & Lemon (& Public Theatre, NY), Abel's Sister, Fen (& Joint Stock/Public Theatre, NY/UK tour).**

Other theatre includes: **People, Schism In England, Juno & The Paycock, A Place with the Pigs** (National); **The Winter's Tale, Pericles, Henry IV Part I & II, The Theban Plays, Artists & Admirers** (RSC); **Roots, Phaedra** (Donmar); **Richard III, The Taming of the Shrew** (Globe); **Love Me Tonight, Out in the Open** (& Birmingham Rep), **The Awakening** (Hampstead); **The Seagull** (Liverpool Playhouse); **The Bald Prima Donna, Medea,** (Leicester Haymarket/Liverpool Playhouse/Almeida); **The Cherry Orchard** (Leicester Haymarket); **The Clearing** (Bush); **Hortensia & The Museum of Dreams** (Finborough); **Road To Mecca** (Arcola); **Five Kinds of Silence** (Lyric, Hammersmith); **John Gabriel Borkman** (English Touring Company); **The Dove** (Croydon Warehouse); **The Triumph of Love** (Almeida/Tour).

Television includes: **Call The Midwife, The Life & Adventures of Nick Nickleby, Spies of Warsaw, Grandma's House, Lark Rise to Candleford, Sense & Sensibility, The Brief, This Little Life, Our Mutual Friend, Kavanagh QC, Casualty, Far from the Madding Crowd, Silent Film, Christmas, A Touch of Frost, A Small Dance, No Bananas, Newshounds, A Village Affair, Bramwell, Loved Up, Skallagrig.**

Film includes: **Effie, West is West, Cass, The Reader, Kinky Boots, Separate Lies, Calendar Girls, The Hours, The Martins, Don Quixote, East is East, Beautiful People, Oscar & Lucinda, Paris By Night, Waiting for the Moon, Leave To Remain, Indian Summer.**

Awards include: **Semana Internacional de Cine Valladolid Espania for Best Actress (East is East); Theatrical Management Association Award for Best Actress (Lucky Dog); Clarence Derwent Award for Best Actress in a Supporting Role (Far Away).**

Miriam Buether (Designer)

For the Royal Court: **The Children, Escaped Alone, In The Republic of Happiness, Sucker Punch, Love & Information, Cock, Get Santa!**

Theatre includes: **The Father** (Tricycle/Theatre Royal, Bath/West End); **Wild** (Hampstead); **Boy, Game, Judgement Day** (Almeida); **Sunny Afternoon** (& Hampstead), **Chariots of Fire** (& Hampstead), **Bend It Like Beckham** (West End); **Measure for Measure, The Trial, Public Enemy, Wild Swans, The Government Inspector, In the Red & Brown Water, The Good Soul Of Szechuan, Generations** (Young Vic); **Decade** (Headlong); **The Effect, Earthquakes in London** (National); **Six Characters in Search of an Author** (Headlong/Chichester Festival/West End); **Guantanamo: Honor Bound to Defend Freedom** (Tricycle/West End/New York/San Francisco).

Opera includes: **Boris Godunov, The Girl of the Golden West** (ENO/Santa Fe Opera); **Anna Nicole** (& New York City Opera), **Il Trittico/Suor Angelica** (Royal Opera House).

Awards include: **Critics' Circle Award for Best Theatre Design (Wild Swans); Evening Standard Award for Best Theatre Design (Earthquakes in London); Evening Standard Award for Best Theatre Design (Sucker Punch).**

Miriam was also awarded the Linbury Prize for Stage Design in 1999.

Deborah Findlay (Sally)

For the Royal Court: **The Children, Escaped Alone, Tom & Viv, Top Girls** (& Off-Broadway), **The Overgrown Path.**

Other theatre includes: **Coriolanus, Moonlight, Madame de Sade, John Gabriel Borkman, The Cut, The Vortex** (Donmar); **The Winslow Boy** (Old Vic); **Timon of Athens, The Winter's Tale, Rules For Living, Stanley** (& Broadway), **The House of Bernarda Alba, The Mandate, Mother Clap's Molly House, Once in a While** (National); **Vincent River** (Off-Broadway); **The Glass Menagerie** (Young Vic); **Like a Fishbone, Keyboard Skills, Commitments** (Bush); **Separate Tables** (Chichester Festival); **The Way of The World, The Crucible** (Sheffield); **Tongue of a Bird, Hedda Gabler** (Almeida); **The Beaux' Stratagem, The Seagull, The Clandestine Marriage** (Tour/West End); **As You Like It, King Lear** (Oxford Stage Company); **Macbeth**

(Nuffield, Southampton); Twelfth Night, The Merchant of Venice, The Three Sisters, The New Inn, The School for Scandal (RSC).

Television includes: **Lovesick, High & Dry, Coalition, Leaving, Poirot, Life in Squares, Torchwood, Gunrush, Lewis, New Tricks, Midsomer Murders, Thin Ice, Cranford, Wives & Daughters, Silent Witness, Anna Karenina, The Family Man, Foyle's War, State of Play.**

Film includes: **Kaleidoscope, Jackie, The Lady in the Van, The Ones Below, Summer, Vanity Fair, Me Without You, The End of the Affair, Jack & Sarah, Truly Madly Deeply.**

Awards include: **Olivier Award for Best Supporting Actress (Stanley); New York Drama League Prize for Outstanding Performance (Stanley); OBIE award (Top Girls).**

James Macdonald (Director)

For the Royal Court: **The Children, Escaped Alone, The Wolf From The Door, Circle Mirror Transformation, Love & Information (& Minetta Lane, NYC); Cock (& Duke, NYC), Drunk Enough to Say I Love You? (& Public, NYC), Dying City, Fewer Emergencies, Lucky Dog, Blood, Blasted, 4.48 Psychosis (& European tour/US tour), Hard Fruit, Real Classy Affair, Cleansed, Ballegangaire, Harry & Me, Simpatico, Blasted, Peaches, Thyestes, Hammett's Apprentice, The Terrible Voice of Satan, Putting Two & Two Together.**

Other theatre includes: **The Chinese Room** (Williamstown Theatre Festival); **Wild, And No More Shall We Part** (& Traverse), **#alww - The Arrest of Ai Weiwei** (Hampstead); **The Father** (Theatre Royal, Bath/Tricycle/West End); **Bakkhai, A Delicate Balance, Judgment Day, The Triumph of Love** (Almeida); **Cloud Nine** (Atlantic, NYC); **Roots** (Donmar); **King Lear, The Book of Grace** (Public, NYC); **Top Girls** (Broadway/MTC, NYC); **Dying City** (Lincoln Center, NYC); **A Number** (NYTW, NYC); **John Gabriel Borkman** (Abbey, Dublin/BAM, NYC); **Dido Queen of Carthage, The Hour We Knew Nothing of Each Other, Exiles** (National); **Glengarry Glen Ross, The Changing Room** (West End); **Troilus und Cressida, Die Kopien** (Schaubuehne, Berlin); **4.48 Psychose** (Burgtheater, Vienna); **The Tempest, Roberto Zucco** (RSC); **Love's Labour's Lost, Richard II** (Royal Exchange, Manchester); **The Rivals** (Nottingham Playhouse); **The Crackwalker** (Gate); **The Seagull** (Crucible, Sheffield); **Miss Julie** (Oldham Coliseum); **Juno & the Paycock, Ice Cream & Hot Fudge, Romeo & Juliet, Fool for Love, Savage/Love, Master Harold & the Boys** (Contact); **Prem** (BAC/Soho Poly).

Opera includes: **A Ring A Lamp A Thing** (Linbury); **Eugene Onegin, Rigoletto** (WNO); **Die Zauberflöte** (Garsington); **Wolf Club Village, Night Banquet** (Almeida Opera); **Oedipus Rex, Survivor from Warsaw** (Royal Exchange, Manchester/Hallé); **Lives of the Great Poisoners** (Second Stride).

Film includes: **A Number.**

James was an Associate Director at the Royal Court from 1992 to 2006 and a NESTA fellow from 2003 to 2006.

Kika Markham (Lena)

For the Royal Court: **Escaped Alone, Tribes, Time Present (& West End), Twelfth Night.**

Other theatre includes: **The Crucible** (Bristol Old Vic); **The Last Yankee** (Print Room); **On the Record** (Arcola); **Women Power & Politics** (Tricycle); **The Permanent Way** (Out of Joint/National); **Homebody/Kabul** (Young Vic); **The Vagina Monologues, The Taming of the Shrew** (& Theatr Clwyd), **Anthony & Cleopatra, Song at Twilight** (West End); **A Wedding Story** (Soho/UK Tour); **Black Sail White Sail** (Gate); **A Bright Room Called Day** (Bush); **Macbeth** (Thorndike); **The Seagull** (Nottingham Playhouse).

Television includes: **Fearless, New Tricks, Mr Selfridge, Secret State, Holby City, Call the Midwife, Einstein & Eddington, Party Animals, Lord Longford, Messiah, The Line of Beauty, Dirty Filthy Love, Born & Bred, The Canterbury Tales: The Man of Law's Tale, The Inspector Lynley Mysteries, Waking the Dead, Touching Evil, The Woman in White, The Bill, The Young Indiana Jones Chronicles, Return of Sherlock Holmes, Double Dare, The Basement.**

Film includes: **Franklyn, Paint It Yellow, The Fever, Esther Khan, Killing Me Softly, Wonderland, A Very British Coup, The Innocent, Outland, Anne & Muriel, Operation Daybreak.**

Awards include: **Clarence Derwent Award for Best Supporting Actress (Song at Twilight).** Kika has written a memoir of her life with Corin Redgrave titled "Our Time of Day".

Peter Mumford (Lighting Designer)

For the Royal Court: **The Children, Escaped Alone, The Wolf From The Door, In The Republic of Happiness, Circle Mirror Transformation, Jumpy (& West End), Our Private Life, Sucker Punch, Drunk Enough To Say I Love You? (& Public Theater, NYC), The Seagull (& Broadway), Love & Information (& Minetta Lane, NYC), Dying City.**

Other theatre includes: **Mr Foote's Other Leg, A Christmas Carol, Women on the Verge of a Nervous Breakdown, Donkey Heart, Stephen Ward, Top Hat** (West End); **Stepping Out** (Theatre Royal, Bath/UK Tour); **Bull** (Young Vic); **Little Eyolf, Ghosts** (& West End/BAM), **Bakkhai** (Almeida); **Long Day's Journey Into Night** (Bristol Old Vic); **High Society, Other Desert Cities** (Old Vic); **King Kong** (Regent, Melbourne); **King Lear** (Chichester Festival/BAM, NYC); **Scenes from an Execution, Bacchai** (National); **Wonderland, The Last Of The Duchess, Enlightenment** (Hampstead).

Opera & Dance includes: **Manon Lescaut (Metropolitan Opera, NYC); Andrea Chénier (Opera North); Carmen (Royal Ballet/Carlos Acosta); The King Dances, Faster, E=mc2, Take Five (Birmingham Royal Ballet); Carmen (Miami City Ballet/Richard Alston); Ein Reigen (Vienna State Ballet); Katya Kabanova (Boston Lyric Opera); Manon Lescaut (Baden Baden); Werther, Madama Butterfly, Faust (Metropolitan Opera); La Traviata (Glyndebourne); The Damnation of Faust, Madame Butterfly (ENO); Pelléas et Mélisande (Mariinsky).**

Awards include: **Olivier Award for Outstanding Achievement in Dance (The Glass Blew In); Olivier Award for Best Lighting Design (Bacchai); Knight of Illumination Award (Sucker Punch); Helpmann Award for Best Lighting (King Kong); Green Room Award for Best Lighting (King Kong).**

In addition to Peter's Lighting Design work, he also designed the sets for Dying City at the Royal Court and Carmen at Miami City Ballet. Peter created the concert staging, design concept plus the lighting and projection design for Wagner's Ring Cycle produced by Opera North, presented at the Royal Festival Hall.

Stella Powell-Jones (Associate Director)

As Associate Director: **The Father (West End/ National Tour).**

As Assistant Director: **Cock (Duke, NYC); Macbeth (Globe); The Fortress of Solitude (Dallas Theatre Center, TX/Public, NYC); The Ugly One (Soho Rep, NYC).**

As Director: **The Healing, 17 Orchard Point (Theater Row, NYC); The Mystery of Love and Sex (Signature, Washington D.C.); Trevor (Circle X, Los Angeles); Wet Glitter (IRT, NYC); Just Right Just Now (Lesser America, NYC); Robin Hood, Bulfinch's Mythology, The Gnadiges Fraulein, Mr. Universe (Williamstown Theatre Festival, Massachusetts); The Eye of the Needle (Courting Drama/Theater Renegade).**

Tariq Rifaat (Production Manager)

For the Royal Court: **The Pride, Tusk Tusk, Cock, Tribes, Choir Boy, The River, Constellations (& West End), The Nether (& West End), The Low Road, God Bless the Child, Fireworks.**

Theatre includes: **Anna Christie (Donmar); Di & Viv & Rose (& West End), Farewell to the Theatre, A Human Being Died That Night, Good People (Hampstead); Twelfth Night, Richard III (West End); The House That Will Not Stand (Tricycle); Minetti (Barbican/Royal Lyceum, Edinburgh); The Red Lion, Evening at the Talkhouse, People Places & Things (& West End), The Suicide, Young Chekhov Season, Amadeus (National).**

Tariq was resident Production Manager at the Royal Court from 2008 to 2015 and is now a Production Manager at the National Theatre.

Christopher Shutt (Sound Designer)

For the Royal Court: **The Sewing Group, Escaped Alone, Love & Information (& New York), Kin, Aunt Dan & Lemon, Bliss, Free Outgoing, The Arsonists, Serious Money, Road.**

Other theatre includes: **St Joan, Faith Healer, Privacy, The Same Deep Water As Me, Philadelphia, Here I Come!, Piaf, The Man Who Had All the Luck, Hecuba (Donmar); Wild (Hampstead); Merchant of Venice (Globe); The Entertainer, The Winter's Tale (West End); The Father (Theatre Royal, Bath/Tricycle/West End); Hamlet, Julius Caesar (Barbican); Bull (Young Vic); Here We Go, The Beaux' Stratagem, Man & Superman, The James Plays (I & II), From Morning to Midnight, Strange Interlude, Timon of Athens, The Last of the Haussmans, The White Guard, Burnt by the Sun, Every Good Boy Deserves Favour, The Hour We Knew Nothing of Each Other, War Horse (& West End), Philistines, Happy Days, Thérèse Raquin, The Seagull, Burn/Chatroom/Citizenship, Coram Boy, A Dream Play, A Minute Too Late, Measure for Measure, Mourning Becomes Elektra, Play Without Words, Machinal (National); The Playboy of the Western World, All About My Mother, Life x 3 (Old Vic); Ruined, Judgement Day (Almeida); Desire Under the Elms, Blasted (Lyric, Hammersmith); A Human Being Died That Night, And No More Shall We Part, For Once (Hampstead); Thyestes (Arcola); Shoes (Sadler's Wells); The Caretaker (& Tricycle), Crave/4:48 Psychosis (Crucible, Sheffield); Oppenheimer (& West End), The Two Gentlemen of Verona, Wendy & Peter Pan, Candide, Twelfth Night, The Comedy of Errors, The Tempest, King Lear, Romeo & Juliet, Noughts & Crosses, King John, Much Ado About Nothing (RSC); Macbeth (Manchester International Festival/ New York); Drum Belly (Abbey); Far Away, A Midsummer Night's Dream (Bristol Old Vic); Good (Royal Exchange, Manchester); Man of Aran (Druid); The House of Special Purpose (Chichester Festival); Little Otik, The Bacchae (National Theatre of Scotland); Riders to the Sea (ENO); A Disappearing Number, The Elephant Vanishes, Mnemonic (& Broadway), The Noise of Time, The Street of Crocodiles, The Three Lives of Lucie Cabrol, The Caucasian Chalk Circle (Complicite); A Human Being Died That Night, Macbeth, All My Sons, The Resistible Rise of Arturo Ui, Happy Days, A Moon for the Misbegotten, Coram Boy, Humble Boy, Not About Nightingales, (Broadway).**

Awards include: **Tony Award for Best Sound Design of a Play (War Horse); Evening Standard Theatre Award (A Disappearing Number); New York Drama Desk Award for Outstanding Sound Design (Mnemonic); New York Drama Desk Award for Outstanding Sound Design (Not About Nightingales).**

June Watson (Vi)

For the Royal Court: **Escaped Alone, Talking to Terrorists (& Out of Joint), Kosher Harry, Sliding with Suzanne (& International Tour), Beside Herself, Saved, Small Change (& National), Life Price, Glasshouses.**

Other theatre includes: **The Father, Mrs Lowry & Son, The Cripple of Inishmaan (& Broadway), Uncle Vanya, Mary Stuart, Smaller (West End); Good People (Hampstead); Before the Party (Almeida); Calendar Girls (UK Tour); The Children's Hour (Royal Exchange, Manchester); Romeo & Juliet (RSC); Scenes from the Big Picture, Our Lady of Sligo, Le Cid, Machinal (National); Streetcar to Tennessee (Young Vic).**

Television includes: **To Walk Invisible, Agatha Raisin, Thirteen, Unforgotten, A Song for Jenny, Holby City, Doctors, Law & Order UK, The Bill, The Street, City of Vice, Clapham Junction, Midsomer Murders.**

Film includes: **The Death of Stalin, The Lady in the Van, Ghost Hunter, 102 Dalmatians, Highlander IV: Endgame.**

Awards include: **Clarence Derwent Award for Best Female in a Supporting Role (The Cripple of Inishmaan & Before The Party).**

Roy Alexander Weise (Assistant Director)

As Director, for the Royal Court: **Primetime 2016, On Fleek, In Smoke, Aperture (Live Lunch).**

As Assistant Director, for the Royal Court: **Escaped Alone, You For Me For You, Hangmen, Primetime 2015, Violence & Son, Who Cares, Liberian Girl.**

As Director, other theatre includes: **The Mountaintop, Plunder, One Million Tiny Plays about Britain (Young Vic); Stone Face (Finborough); Palindrome (Miniaturists); The Man in the Green Jacket (Jermyn Street); SKEEN! (Ovalhouse); Invisible Mice (Lyric, Hammersmith); Seventeen (Rose Bruford College); Chameleon (Unicorn).**

As Assistant Director, other theatre includes: **Albion, We Are Proud to Present... (Bush); Public Enemy, Hamlet, The Government Inspector (Young Vic); The Serpent's Tooth (Shoreditch Town Hall/ Almeida/Talawa); Lulu (Rose Bruford College).**

THE ROYAL COURT THEATRE

The Royal Court Theatre is the writers' theatre. It is a leading force in world theatre for energetically cultivating writers – undiscovered, emerging and established.

Through the writers, the Royal Court is at the forefront of creating restless, alert, provocative theatre about now. We open our doors to the unheard voices and free thinkers that, through their writing, change our way of seeing.

Over 120,000 people visit the Royal Court in Sloane Square, London, each year and many thousands more see our work elsewhere through transfers to the West End and New York, UK and international tours, digital platforms, our residencies across London, and our site-specific work. Through all our work we strive to inspire audiences and influence future writers with radical thinking and provocative discussion.

The Royal Court's extensive development activity encompasses a diverse range of writers and artists and includes an ongoing programme of writers' attachments, readings, workshops and playwriting groups. Twenty years of the International Department's pioneering work around the world means the Royal Court has relationships with writers on every continent.

Within the past sixty years, John Osborne, Samuel Beckett, Arnold Wesker, Ann Jellicoe, Howard Brenton and David Hare have started their careers at the Court.

Many others including Caryl Churchill, Athol Fugard, Mark Ravenhill, Simon Stephens, debbie tucker green, Sarah Kane - and, more recently, Lucy Kirkwood, Nick Payne, Penelope Skinner and Alistair McDowall - have followed.

The Royal Court has produced many iconic plays from Laura Wade's **Posh** to Jez Butterworth's **Jerusalem** and Martin McDonagh's **Hangmen**.

Royal Court plays from every decade are now performed on stage and taught in classrooms and universities across the globe.

It is because of this commitment to the writer that we believe there is no more important theatre in the world than the Royal Court.

Supported using public funding by

**ARTS COUNCIL
ENGLAND**

ROYAL

SPRING / SUMMER 2017

28 Feb – 1 Apr
a profoundly affectionate, passionate devotion to someone *(-noun)*
Written and directed by debbie tucker green

7 Mar – 8 Apr
Patrick Milling Smith, Barbara Broccoli, Michael Wilson,
Brian Carmody and the Royal Court Theatre
in association with Complicite
the kid stays in the picture
Based on the life story of Robert Evans
Directed by Simon McBurney

19 Apr – 6 May
nuclear war
Text by Simon Stephens
Directed by Imogen Knight

24 Apr – 20 May
Royal Court Theatre and Sonia Friedman Productions
In association with Neal Street Productions
the ferryman
By Jez Butterworth
Directed by Sam Mendes

10 May – 20 May
MANWATCHING
by an anonymous woman

25 May – 24 Jun
Royal Court Theatre and Sherman Theatre Cardiff
killology
By Gary Owen
Directed by Rachel O'Riordan

3 Jun – 8 Jul
anatomy of a suicide
By Alice Birch
Directed by Katie Mitchell

21 Jul – 9 Sep
road
By Jim Cartwright
Directed by John Tiffany

Tickets from £12 0207 565 5000
royalcourttheatre.com

Supported using public funding by
**ARTS COUNCIL
ENGLAND**

Sloane Square London, SW1W 8AS
🐦 royalcourt 📘 royalcourttheatre
⊖ Sloane Square ⇌ Victoria Station

COURT

ROYAL

Catch the Royal Court Theatre production of

ESCAPED ALONE

by Caryl Churchill   on tour in 2017

Wed 15 – Sun 26 Feb
BROOKLYN ACADEMY OF MUSIC (BAM)
718.636.4100 | BAM.org

Tue 7 – Sat 11 Mar
THE LOWRY, SALFORD QUAYS
0843 208 6010* | thelowry.com/drama

Tue 14 – Sat 18 Mar
CAMBRIDGE ARTS THEATRE
01223 503333 | cambridgeartstheatre.com

Wed 22 – Sun 26 Mar
BRISTOL OLD VIC
0117 987 7877 | bristololdvic.org.uk

Tickets may be subject to a booking and/or transaction fee. * Calls to 08 numbers will cost up to 7p per minute, plus your phone company's access charge. See venue website for further details.

royalcourttheatre.com

Supported using public funding by
**ARTS COUNCIL
ENGLAND**

Sloane Square London, SW1W 8AS
🐦 royalcourt 🅵 royalcourttheatre
🚇 Sloane Square 🚆 Victoria Station

ROYAL COURT SUPPORTERS

The Royal Court is a registered charity and not-for-profit company. We need to raise £1.7 million every year in addition to our core grant from the Arts Council and our ticket income to achieve what we do.

We have significant and longstanding relationships with many generous organisations and individuals who provide vital support. Royal Court supporters enable us to remain the writers' theatre, find stories from everywhere and create theatre for everyone.

We can't do it without you.

The Genesis Foundation supports the Royal Court's work with International Playwrights.
Bloomberg supports Beyond the Court.
Jerwood Charitable Foundation supports emerging writers through the Jerwood New Playwrights series.
The Pinter Commission is given annually by his widow, Lady Antonia Fraser, to support a new commission at the Royal Court.

Supported using public funding by
ARTS COUNCIL ENGLAND

Remember the Royal Court in your will and help to ensure that our future is as iconic as our past.

Every gift, whatever the amount, will help us maintain and care for the building, support the next generation of playwrights starting out in their career, deliver our education programme and put our plays on the stage.

LEAVE A LEGACY

To discuss leaving a legacy to the Royal Court, please contact:

Charlotte Christesen, Head of Individual Giving (Maternity Cover), Royal Court Theatre, Sloane Square, London, SW1W 8AS

Email: charlottechristesen@royalcourttheatre.com
Tel: 020 7565 5060

ESCAPED ALONE

Caryl Churchill

'I only am escaped alone to tell thee.'
Book of Job. Moby Dick.

Characters

SALLY
VI
LENA
MRS JARRETT

They are all at least seventy.

Place

Sally's backyard.

Several unmatching chairs. Maybe one's a kitchen chair.

Time

Summer afternoon.

A number of afternoons but the action is continuous.

1.

MRS J   I'm walking down the street and there's a door in the fence open and inside are three women I've seen before.

VI   Don't look now but there's someone watching us.

LENA   Is it that woman?

SALLY   Is that you, Mrs Jarrett?

MRS J   So I go in.

SALLY   Rosie locked out in the rain

VI   forgot her key

SALLY   climbed over

LENA   lucky to have neighbours who

SALLY   such a high wall

VI   this is Rosie her granddaughter

MRS J   I've a son, Frank

VI   I've a son

MRS J   suffers from insomnia

VI   doesn't come very often. But Thomas

LENA   that's her nephew

SALLY   he'd knock up the shelves in no time

VI   a big table

SALLY   grain of the wood

VI   a table like that would last a lifetime

SALLY	an heirloom
LENA	except we all eat off our laps
MRS J	nothing like a table
LENA	I like a table
VI	all have each other's keys because there's no way round and anyway I couldn't climb
MRS J	unless you lose them
VI	no I hang them all on a nail
SALLY	in a teapot
VI	teapot?
SALLY	Elsie puts them in and takes them out
LENA	down the floorboards
VI	only use bags in mugs
SALLY	holds your finger and then takes one step and down she goes.
LENA	Barney never out of his phone
VI	I'd have been the same
LENA	looking pale
VI	whole worlds in your pocket
LENA	little bit worried about Kevin and Mary, never hear an endearment
SALLY	but nobody ever knows
MRS J	you'd be surprised what goes on
LENA	twenty years in June
VI	we had to wear hats
SALLY	a pink one and I didn't
VI	so you gave it to Angela

SALLY	I'd forgotten Angela
LENA	shadows under her eyes
VI	ended up with a green one and it didn't suit you
LENA	I could never say a word of course.
VI	And Maisie, never so happy
LENA	that's her niece
SALLY	quantum
VI	I can't really follow
SALLY	I can't even add up
LENA	they don't add up any more
VI	particles and waves I can manage but after that
SALLY	always good at sums as a child, she'd say two big numbers
VI	and while we were carrying things in our head
LENA	I needed a pencil
SALLY	she'd say the answer and it was always right
MRS J	I could always make change quick with the shillings and pence
VI	we'd be the ones got it wrong
LENA	easier now it's decimal
SALLY	always right.
LENA	And Vera

MRS J   Four hundred thousand tons of rock paid for by
          senior executives split off the hillside to smash
          through the roofs, each fragment onto the
          designated child's head. Villages were buried and
          new communities of survivors underground
          developed skills of feeding off the dead where
          possible and communicating with taps and groans.
          Instant celebrities rose on ropes to the light of
          flashes. Time passed. Rats were eaten by those
          who still had digestive systems, and mushrooms
          were traded for urine. Babies were born and
          quickly became blind. Some groups lost their
          sexuality while others developed a new morality of
          constant fucking with any proximate body. A
          young woman crawling from one society to the
          other became wedged, only her head reaching her
          new companions. Stories of those above ground
          were told and retold till there were myths of the
          husband who cooked feasts, the wife who swam
          the ocean, the gay lover who could fly, the child
          who read minds, the talking dog. Prayers were said
          to them and various sects developed with tolerance
          and bitter hatred. Songs were sung until dry
          throats caused the end of speech. Torrential rain
          leaked through cracks and flooded the tunnels
          enabling screams at last before drownings.
          Survivors were now solitary and went insane at
          different rates.

2.

SALLY	corner shop
LENA	don't like the
VI	mini Tesco
LENA	bit far
MRS J	used to be the fish and chip shop
VI	that other one's gone
SALLY	the old grocer
VI	I'd do a shop for seventeen shillings
LENA	so what's that in
MRS J	fifteen's seventyfive p
VI	but we earned nothing too
SALLY	so who does the shopping if you can't go out?
LENA	I do go
VI	is Kevin a help?
SALLY	I could always
VI	but it's good for you to go yourself
SALLY	good to get out
LENA	I do get out
SALLY	you're here
LENA	it's not easy
SALLY	antique shop now but in between it was that café
VI	it was never a café

SALLY	the Blue something, an animal
MRS J	I been there
SALLY	Hedgehog, something unlikely
VI	I don't think so
SALLY	maybe it was when
LENA	oh
SALLY	that would be it of course
VI	I did miss a few things when I was away
MRS J	away was you?
LENA	just a little while
VI	six years
SALLY	that's what it was then, Blue Antelope
VI	antique shops now but down the other end
SALLY	yes three shops boarded up
VI	that's the nail parlour and the old dentist
SALLY	did you ever go?
VI	he was terrible
SALLY	he was such a bad
VI	'this might just trouble you a little'
SALLY	oh my god
VI	half an hour to get there but so much better
LENA	I should go to the dentist
SALLY	a checkup
LENA	it must be five years
MRS J	you don't want toothache
LENA	it's just one more thing you have to do, one thing after another, I can't seem to

SALLY	I could always go with you
LENA	if I go
SALLY	or do some shopping
VI	it's good she gets out herself
LENA	I do get out
SALLY	and the chicken nuggets closed down
VI	that was the ironmongers
SALLY	no in between it was the health shop
LENA	a hammer and a spade
VI	there must be quite a few things I missed
SALLY	not really, it all goes by, I can't remember those years specially
VI	remember what was happening where I was of course
SALLY	yes of course
VI	though it gets to be a blur because it's all a bit the same
SALLY	it must have been
VI	unless there was an excitement like a fight
MRS J	fights was there?
VI	or love affairs
LENA	I do get out it's just difficult

MRS J   First the baths overflowed as water was
          deliberately wasted in a campaign to punish the
          thirsty. Swimming pools engulfed the leisure
          centres and coffee ran down the table legs. Rivers
          flowed back towards their tributaries and up the
          streams to what had been trickles in moss. Ponies
          climbed to high ground and huddled with the
          tourists. Yawls, ketches, kayaks, canoes, schooners,
          planks, dinghies, lifebelts and upturned umbrellas,
          swimming instructors and lilos, rubber ducks and
          pumice stone floated on the stock market. Waves
          engulfed ferris wheels and drowned bodies were
          piled up to block doors. Then the walls of water
          came from the sea. Villages vanished and cities
          relocated to their rooftops. Sometimes children fell
          down the sewage chutes but others caught seagulls
          with kites. Some died of thirst, some of drinking
          the water. When the flood receded thousands
          stayed on the roofs fed by helicopter while heroes
          and bonded workers shovelled the muck into
          buckets that were stored in the flood museums.

3.

VI	Parallel universes
SALLY	fiction
VI	scientists
SALLY	makes good stories
VI	second series
LENA	I'm watching the third
SALLY	does Elliott
MRS J	don't tell us
SALLY	too many universes for me
LENA	when I stay home I watch
VI	you've seen everything
SALLY	but you're feeling better
LENA	it just drops away, you wake up one morning and it's all right
SALLY	amazing
LENA	like a different world
VI	universe
MRS J	I don't like Elliott
VI	the way he looks at his wife
LENA	but you're meant to think that
SALLY	I do think that, I don't care
VI	and now the money

SALLY	Ursula's nasty
VI	I'm sorry for Ursula
SALLY	I think it's going to be Ursula
MRS J	four husbands
LENA	they want you to think that
VI	loved her in the first series
LENA	exactly
SALLY	but universes to get your mind round
LENA	the third series
VI	and the very very small
SALLY	yes our bodies
VI	millions of little creatures
LENA	makes my flesh creep
VI	fleas on a cat
LENA	microbes on a flea
VI	oh
LENA	oh
VI	sorry
LENA	look what you've done
MRS J	what's she done?
LENA	we don't mention
VI	are you all right?
MRS J	what, fleas?
VI	no
LENA	cats
VI	shh

LENA	are you all right?
SALLY	yes I'm fine thank you
VI	sorry I'm so sorry
SALLY	the third series
LENA	particles
VI	though mind you are we helping by never saying?
LENA	don't start that
SALLY	it's all right, you needn't
VI	shouldn't we just say it, say black and white, tabby, longhaired, shorthaired, siamese
MRS J	I've got a lovely tabby but he's a tom so
LENA	stop it
VI	expose her to it and nothing bad happens and she gets used to nothing bad
LENA	stop it
VI	I'm helping
MRS J	is she going to faint?
SALLY	no no I'm
LENA	see?
VI	I'm sorry I just get
SALLY	I know it's stupid
VI	no
SALLY	I know you hate me sometimes
VI	no, I
LENA	see?
SALLY	you just need to face
VI	I need to face?
SALLY	how unpleasant you can be

LENA   see?

VI   oh it's me now, it's always someone

LENA   stop it

MRS J   let's hear it

SALLY   it doesn't bother me

VI   oh let's not

SALLY   it's fine

VI   I know I shouldn't

SALLY   so tell us about the third series

MRS J   don't tell us about the third series

LENA   I'll just hint that Elliott

VI   don't say it

MRS J   The chemicals leaked through cracks in the money.
The first symptoms were irritability and nausea.
Domestic violence increased and there were
incidents on the underground. School absenteeism
tripled and ninetyseven schools were taken into
special measures. Dog owners cleared up their pets'
vomit or risked a fine. Miscarriages were frequent
leading to an increase of opportunities in grief
counselling. Birth deformities outpaced the
immigration of plastic surgeons. Gas masks were
available on the NHS with a three month waiting
time and privately in a range of colours.
Sometimes the cancers began in the lungs and
sometimes on the fingertips or laptops. The
remaining citizens were evacuated to camps in
northern Canada where they were sprayed and
victimised, and the city was left to sick foxes, who
soon abandoned it for lack of dustbins.

4.

LENA	So how many noughts
VI	a billion has nine
SALLY	no
VI	a trillion
SALLY	a billion has twelve
VI	no, we adopted the American
SALLY	are you saying a billion isn't a million million?
VI	a thousand million now, and a trillion
SALLY	oh I don't like that
MRS J	what's a zillion?
VI	and then of course you get a googol and a googolplex, which isn't the same as
LENA	a zillion's what you say, is it a real
VI	three Brazilians dead and President Bush said Oh no, remind me how many is a brazilian
SALLY	he's taken the place of moron
LENA	moron?
SALLY	when I was a child Little Moron jokes for anything stupid, what did the Little Moron say when he
VI	what did he say?
LENA	no one says moron
SALLY	they keep having to change what you can say because whatever word they use becomes

VI	did we ever say moron for jokes? is it American or
LENA	but you can't even make that kind of joke not about mentally
SALLY	Irish for a long time, Irish jokes
MRS J	'no blacks no dogs no Irish'
SALLY	I remember that
VI	and we weren't even that shocked
LENA	we do shock easier
VI	but you have to have jokes about stupid things someone might do because anyone might, it's funny
LENA	you can't have a class of people
SALLY	you could have yourself
VI	you could have me
SALLY	what did I say when I jumped off the top of
VI	don't the comedians do that, they make themselves
SALLY	but of course we know they're clever.
LENA	So in other countries do they have that?
VI	jokes about being stupid?
LENA	making out it's some neighbour who's
SALLY	you always get people hating their neighbours
VI	yes the closer they are
SALLY	Serbs and Croats, French and English
LENA	there's history though
SALLY	but anyone everyone outside thinks is the same
VI	Catholics and Protestants, Sunni and Shia
MRS J	Arsenal and Tottenham

SALLY	there you are
LENA	Cain and Abel
VI	did Abel make jokes about Cain being stupid and that's why he killed him?
LENA	odd they needed a story about how killing started because
SALLY	chimpanzees
LENA	but you do wonder why of course so you make a story
VI	easily done I found
SALLY	different each time
VI	I don't know why, I never knew why
MRS J	found it easy did you?
LENA	never mind that
SALLY	not always easy and a lot of men in the war never fired their guns because
VI	no it's all right, she can know
MRS J	what can I know?
VI	tell her, go on
LENA	she accidentally
SALLY	a long time ago
LENA	accidentally killed her husband
VI	not accidentally
LENA	in self defence
MRS J	how did you do that?
VI	kitchen knife happened to be in my hand
LENA	just bad luck really

VI	so when I hit back
MRS J	so that was all right was it, self defence
SALLY	more complicated
LENA	the lawyers
SALLY	manslaughter
VI	six years, which was half
MRS J	still a long time
VI	the first two years
LENA	things do speed up
SALLY	everything does
MRS J	you get used to it
SALLY	so that can be good but when it's your whole life speeding up
LENA	don't start on that
SALLY	I'd like to have time travel
VI	knock knock
LENA	who's there?
VI	Dr
SALLY	that's a six year old's joke.

MRS J   The hunger began when eighty per cent of food was diverted to tv programmes. Commuters watched breakfast on iPlayer on their way to work. Smartphones were distributed by charities when rice ran out, so the dying could watch cooking. The entire food stock of Newcastle was won by lottery ticket and the winner taken to a 24 hour dining room where fifty chefs chopped in relays and the public voted on what he should eat next. Cars were traded for used meat. Children fell asleep in class and didn't wake up. The obese sold slices of themselves until hunger drove them to eat their own rashers. Finally the starving stormed the tv centres and were slaughtered and smoked in large numbers. Only when cooking shows were overtaken by sex with football teams did cream trickle back to the shops and rice was airlifted again.

5.

VI	People always want to fly
LENA	fly like a bird
SALLY	that's always the favourite, what would you like
LENA	invisible
VI	languages, I'd like to be able to speak every
SALLY	but we do fly now
MRS J	planes isn't the same
VI	go to any country at all and understand
SALLY	and nobody looks out of the window
LENA	watching the screens
VI	I do like getting all those movies I never
SALLY	looking down on clouds
LENA	yes what would Julius Caesar have thought or
SALLY	and they make it like being in a very unpleasant room
VI	try to make you forget you're up in the air
LENA	because it could be frightening being up in the air
SALLY	because that's not what people mean by flying
VI	flying like a bird in the sky
LENA	but if people could, if we all
VI	that's no good
LENA	imagine the crowds
SALLY	at rush hour

LENA	separate lanes
SALLY	flocks
VI	like starlings, that would be good, all those shapes
LENA	flocks of pigeons, they seem to change colour
SALLY	no we wouldn't have that sense of each other, we'd keep bumping
VI	but what people want is fly by yourself
LENA	straight up like a lark
VI	or hover like what?
LENA	a kestrel
VI	kestrel yes
LENA	or an eagle
VI	soar like an eagle
MRS J	I wouldn't want to be a pigeon
VI	we're not being birds we're us but able to
SALLY	pigeons are like rats
LENA	pigeons are not
VI	looking down from above
SALLY	like drones with cameras
LENA	Barney's got one, remote control, you can see as if you're
VI	I hate that because they bomb and they're not in danger
LENA	it's just a toy
SALLY	is it all right to bomb if you are in danger?
VI	but no it's not the seeing it's the sensation
LENA	soaring and diving

SALLY   like swimming under water really going up and
               down

VI   no only if you can scuba

LENA   hate putting my head under water

VI   birds is better than fish

MRS J   I wouldn't want to be a fish

LENA   or being invisible is the one I'd like

SALLY   all this about birds, I don't quite like about birds
               because birds leads to cats, pigeons leads to cats, cat
               among the pigeons, next door's tabby had a pigeon
               such flapping and couldn't kill it, wouldn't, just
               played about kept grabbing it again and the bird
               was maimed someone had to ugh, and pigeons like
               rats leads to cats rats cats rats are filthy plague
               everywhere, only how many feet from a rat, and
               pigeons are filthy, rats are filthy, cats are filthy their
               bites are poison they bite you and the bite festers,
               but that's not it that's not it I know that's just an
               excuse to give a reason I know I've no reason I
               know it's just cats cats themselves are the horror
               because they're cats and I have to keep them out I
               have to make sure I never think about a cat because
               if I do I have to make sure there's no cats and they
               could be anywhere they could get in a window I
               have to go round the house and make sure all the
               windows are locked and I don't know if I checked
               properly I can't remember I was too frightened to
               notice I have to go round the windows again I have
               to go round the windows again back to the kitchen
               back to the bedroom back to the kitchen back to the
               bedroom the bathroom back to the kitchen back to
               the door, the door might blow open if it's windy
               even if it's not windy suppose the postman was
               putting a large packet and pushed the door and it
               came open because it wasn't properly shut and then
               a cat because they can get through very very small

and once they're in they could be anywhere they could be under the bed in the wardrobe up on the top shelf with the winter sweaters that would be a place for a cat to sleep or in a wastepaper basket or under the cushions on the sofa or in the cupboard with the saucepans or in the cupboard with the food a cat could curl up on the cans of tomatoes a cat could be in with the jam and honey a cat could be in the biscuit tin, a cat could be in the fridge in the freezer in the salad drawer in the box of cheese in the broom cupboard the mop bucket a cat could be in the oven the top oven under the lid of the casserole in a box of matches behind a picture under a rug back to the bedroom a cat could be under the bed in the duvet in the pillowcase in the wardrobe a cat could be in a shoe on a hanger under my dress in a woolly hat inside a coat sleeve a cat could be in any of the drawers so I tip them all out and shake every – cat behind the books on the shelf behind the dvds a cat could be in the teapot with the keys a cat could be on the ceiling a cat could be on top of the door a cat could be behind me a cat could be under my hand when I put out my hand. I need someone to say there's no cats, I need to say to someone do you smell cat, I need to say do you think there's any way a cat could have got in, and they have to say of course not, they have to say of course not, I have to believe them, it has to be someone I believe, I have to believe they're not just saying it, I have to believe they know there are no cats, I have to believe there are no cats. And then briefly the joy of that.

LENA   Eagles you get eagles as national

VI   eagles are fascist

LENA   America has the eagle

VI   well

MRS J   I wouldn't mind being an eagle

SALLY   very often fascist

LENA   shame for the eagle really, it little knows

VI   an eagle wouldn't have much empathy

SALLY   nor would a blackbird come to that

VI   you don't get blackbirds as national

LENA   do religions have birds?

VI   dove of peace

SALLY   sacred ibis

LENA   you could have bird rituals

SALLY   scattering of birdseed

VI   bird calls by the congregation

LENA   holy ghost of course that gets pictured sometimes as

SALLY   that's the dove of peace

VI   I thought the holy ghost was invisible

LENA   I'd rather be invisible myself.

MRS J   The wind developed by property developers
           started as breezes on cheeks and soon turned
           heads inside out. The army fired nets to catch
           flying cars but most spun by with dozens clinging
           and shrieking, dropping off slowly. Buildings
           migrated from London to Lahore, Kyoto to
           Kansas City, and survivors were interned for
           having no travel documents. Some in the
           whirlwind went higher and higher, the airsick
           families taking selfies in case they could ever share
           them. Shanty towns were cleared. Pets rained from
           the sky. A kitten became famous.

6.

All sing **SALLY**, **VI** *and* **LENA** *in harmony.* **MRS JARRETT** *joins in the melody. They are singing for themselves in the garden, not performing to the audience.*

MRS J   The illness started when children drank sugar
            developed from monkeys. Hair fell out, feet
            swelled, organs atrophied. Hairs blowing in the
            wind rapidly passed round the world. When they
            fell into the ocean cod died and fishermen blew up
            each other's boats. Planes with sick passengers
            were diverted to Antarctica. Some got into bed
            with their dead, others locked the doors and ran
            till they fell down. Volunteers and conscripts over
            seven nursed the sick and collected bodies.
            Governments cleansed infected areas and made
            deals with allies to bomb each other's capitals.
            Presidents committed suicide. The last survivors
            had immunity and the virus mutated,
            exterminating plankton.

7.

SALLY	I miss work
VI	I don't miss work at all
SALLY	you're learning Spanish
VI	you're in love
SALLY	a little
MRS J	in love are you?
VI	your job was far
SALLY	could be very boring of course
VI	no all the people and all
SALLY	yes but endless colds coughs coughs sore throats coughs
VI	'antibiotics please'
SALLY	and of course you have to be alert
VI	because sometimes
SALLY	you don't want to miss cancer
VI	did you ever?
SALLY	terrible occasion
MRS J	I go to that Dr Meadows
SALLY	reliable though
MRS J	but you can't get an appointment
VI	envy you doing good
SALLY	made your clients happy

MRS J	what did you
VI	hairdresser
MRS J	cut my own hair, cut my husband's hair
SALLY	tell you their troubles
VI	they did
MRS J	didn't look very good mind
SALLY	and you didn't have to fix the troubles just fix the hair
VI	that's true
SALLY	while I was supposed to fix
VI	and you could sometimes
SALLY	sometimes I could
VI	because hair's a bit trivial
SALLY	yes but you can feel quite new with a different
VI	or miserable if you don't like it
SALLY	the first day or two
VI	kept coming back every couple of days
SALLY	shorter and shorter?
VI	shorter, different colours, I finally had to
MRS J	the hair wasn't the problem
VI	it wasn't the problem
SALLY	and you really don't miss it
VI	I do now we're talking about
SALLY	though I do enjoy the days
VI	yes having the afternoons
MRS J	when I was a lollipop lady a few years back

SALLY	that's afternoon work of course and morning and lunchtime
MRS J	give it up after a month
LENA	I couldn't keep on
VI	you loved that office
LENA	I did
VI	such a highflying
LENA	some days it would be all right for weeks but then I'd find it coming down again. You're so far away from people at the next desk. Email was better than speaking. It's down now. Why can't I just? I just can't. I sat on the bed this morning and didn't stand up till lunchtime. The air was too thick. It's hard to move, it's hard to see why you'd move. It's not so bad in the afternoon, I got myself here. I don't like it here. I've no interest. Why talk about that? Why move your mouth and do talking? Why see anyone? Why know about anyone? It was half past three and all this time later it's twentyfive to four. If I think about a place I could be where there's something nice like the sea that would be worse because the sea would be the same as an empty room so it's better to be in the empty room because then there's fewer things to mean nothing at all. I'd rather hear something bad than something good. I'd rather hear nothing. It's still just the same. It's just the same. It's the same.
SALLY	Your medication doesn't seem very

VI	do you take it?
LENA	it's not an easy thing to
SALLY	not a sprained ankle
MRS J	I had my hips done
VI	and is that
MRS J	two new hips I can walk all day
SALLY	my knee
VI	my back doing hair on my feet all day
SALLY	yes at least I sat
VI	exactly
SALLY	but then I ran
VI	I missed it when I had to stop
MRS J	was that when you was
VI	six years
MRS J	did you go back to hair after?
VI	not the same place, it was never such a good
SALLY	you did several different
VI	out of work completely a long time
MRS J	not fair because it was just self defence was it
VI	it was
LENA	not fair really
SALLY	more complicated
LENA	self defence
SALLY	fair enough really
LENA	you think?
SALLY	because if I'd said

LENA	said what?
SALLY	said what happened
LENA	what happened?
SALLY	it was complicated
MRS J	you was there was you?
SALLY	in the kitchen
VI	you'd had a drink of course
SALLY	we all had, that's why
VI	are you saying
SALLY	I'm just saying I didn't quite
VI	what? come on what? are you saying
SALLY	I didn't tell it quite how it was because
VI	you did
SALLY	no because I took into account what he was like
LENA	it wasn't murder
SALLY	could have been that's all I'm saying if I hadn't
VI	if you hadn't what?
SALLY	hadn't said it in a way that worked out
MRS J	lied in the witness box did you?
SALLY	she's my friend, of course I
VI	you thought you were lying
SALLY	I thought I was economical
VI	you think I murdered him?
SALLY	it's not a matter really of defining
VI	you think I'm a murderer?

SALLY	it doesn't really
VI	all this time you've thought
SALLY	it was so long ago
VI	you think
SALLY	I don't care if you are
VI	I care
SALLY	so long ago
VI	you think
SALLY	look I'm sorry
VI	no what
SALLY	sorry, I shouldn't have
VI	what
SALLY	I don't know what I mean even
LENA	what did you say?
SALLY	I don't even know what I said any more
MRS J	what did you see?
SALLY	certainly don't know what I saw any more
VI	you think I'm a murderer
SALLY	maybe you were I don't know do you think you're a murderer
VI	no
SALLY	okay so maybe you weren't
VI	I don't remember either
MRS J	you don't remember what you
VI	no it's gone
SALLY	there you are then.

VI	I missed cutting hair and I missed food
LENA	prison food
VI	not that I'm much of a cook
MRS J	Frank can cook
VI	I missed snacks in prison and I missed apples

MRS J Fire broke out in ten places at once. Four cases of arson by children and politicians, three of spontaneous combustion of the markets, two of sunshine, one supposed by believers to be a punishment by God for gender dysphoria. It swept through saplings, petrol stations, prisons, dryads and books. Fires were lit to stop the fires and consumed squirrels, firefighters and shoppers. Cars sped from one furnace to another. Houses exploded. Some shot flaming swans, some shot their children. Finally the wind drove the fire to the ocean, where salt water made survivors faint. The blackened area was declared a separate country with zero population, zero growth and zero politics. Charred stumps were salvaged for art and biscuits.

8.

VI	Thomas finished the table
SALLY	love to see it
VI	sit round it before it goes
LENA	bought by some rich
VI	not rich rich not as if it was art
SALLY	art's ridiculous
VI	they buy it just so they can sell it they don't even look
SALLY	Rosie paints very
VI	just for yourself
LENA	and photographs I've always liked
SALLY	easy with phones
LENA	pictures of seabirds, gannets
MRS J	what's gannets?
VI	black, hold their wings out
LENA	that's cormorants
VI	puffins are the ones with beaks, I've never seen
SALLY	you'd have to go somewhere with rocks
LENA	gannets are big and white
MRS J	like a gull
LENA	bigger

SALLY	not like an albatross
VI	albatross round your neck
LENA	fly for years and years and never land.
VI	Birds can be frightening
SALLY	birds?
VI	if they swoop down
MRS J	no that's bats, they get in your hair
SALLY	they don't really
LENA	I was told as a child
SALLY	bats are worse because they zigzag
VI	'bat bat come under my hat, I'll give you a slice of bacon'
LENA	what's that?
VI	I don't know, I just know it
LENA	you'd hardly want it under your hat if you don't even like birds.
SALLY	Elsie chases birds
LENA	Elsie the dog?
VI	Elsie the dog's been dead five years
SALLY	Elsie the baby.
LENA	Dinner with Kevin and Mary
SALLY	did you get an impression
LENA	very cheerful, delicious lamb
SALLY	enjoy cooking sometimes
MRS J	Frank likes a lamb chop
LENA	I do love a kitchen

SALLY   my grandmother's kitchen

LENA   mine's more of a cupboard

SALLY   mine needs a coat of paint

LENA   would Rosie do it?

SALLY   do it myself, just need to make time

MRS J   I can't go up a ladder

LENA   that same dark orange or maybe

VI   I can't love a kitchen, I can't love a kitchen any
         more, if you've killed someone in a kitchen you're
         not going to love that kitchen, I lost that flat, even
         the kitchen where I am now reminds me of that
         kitchen, completely different colour, the cooker's on
         the other wall, and the window, but maybe it's the
         smell of food cooking, it's meat does it, cooking
         meat, the blood if it's rare, we don't often have
         meat, when you've cut somebody and seen the
         blood you don't feel the same, when he fell down
         you think oh good oh good and then you think
         that's a mistake, take that back, the horror happens
         then, keep that out, the horror is the whole thing is
         never the same, he's never a person alive
         somewhere any more, never the same with my son
         is the worst thing never forgive me how do you talk
         to a twelve year old when you've killed his father
         you can't explain everything the whole marriage
         what it's been like you don't want to make him hate
         his father you do want to make him hate his father
         but it wouldn't be right you don't want him to think
         you're someone who would try to make him hate
         his father, he was twelve, he'd visit me, it's hard to
         talk to a teenager if you're not seeing him all the
         time you need to be saying things like tidy your
         room have you done your homework do you want
         to watch a movie, I thought he'd be completely
         grown up but I got time off you have to do good

behaviour, six years he was eighteen he was grown up he was living by himself he'd moved up north he's got a life I'm glad he's got a life, he's got a new partner again he phones sometimes, at least he phones, that's the worst thing even worse than the blood and the thrashing about and what went wrong that's a horror but the horror goes on not seeing him he's got a life, it comes over me sometimes in the kitchen or in the night if I wake up sometimes if it's hot that's worse I can't breathe properly it all comes back in the night, but you get up in the morning and that's better put the kettle on but it's always there not there in the kitchen it's always there.

LENA	Maisie's a good cook
VI	I'm lucky with Maisie
SALLY	all those nieces
VI	I'm lucky with all those
LENA	Maisie bakes
VI	yes but not crazy baking
LENA	a nice sponge
VI	she'd do a birthday cake for her sisters.
SALLY	Rosie's going to China
VI	Rosie?
LENA	holiday or?
SALLY	university
VI	will she learn Mandarin?
LENA	always wanted to go to Japan
SALLY	get to Tesco first
VI	that's nasty
SALLY	no

VI   yes

SALLY   joke

VI   ha

LENA   I thought it was funny.

MRS J   Terrible rage terrible rage terrible rage terrible
            rage terrible rage terrible rage terrible rage terrible
            rage terrible rage terrible rage terrible rage terrible
            rage terrible rage terrible rage terrible rage terrible
            rage terrible rage terrible rage terrible rage terrible
            rage terrible rage terrible rage terrible rage terrible
            rage terrible rage

VI   Why did the chicken not cross the road?

SALLY   why did the chicken not cross the road?

VI   a car was coming

SALLY   that's just silly.

LENA   The sun's gone

VI   this time of day

SALLY   this time of year the shadow comes up earlier

LENA   still it's nice

VI   always nice to be here

MRS J   I like it here

SALLY   afternoons like this.

MRS J   And then I said thanks for the tea and I went
            home.

            End.

Other works by Caryl Churchill, published by Nick Hern Books

Light Shining in Buckinghamshire
Traps
Cloud Nine
Icecream
Mad Forest
The Skriker
Thyestes (translated from Seneca)
Hotel
This is a Chair
Blue Heart
Far Away
A Number
A Dream Play (translated from Strindberg)
Drunk Enough to Say I Love You?
Bliss (translated from Olivier Choinière)
Seven Jewish Children – a play for Gaza
Love and Information
Ding Dong the Wicked
Here We Go

Collections

Plays: Three
    A Mouthful of Birds (with David Lan)
    Icecream
    Mad Forest
    Lives of the Great Poisoners (with Orlando Gough and Ian Spink)
    The Skriker
    Thyestes

Plays: Four
    Hotel
    This is a Chair
    Blue Heart
    Far Away
    A Number
    A Dream Play (translated from Strindberg)
    Drunk Enough to Say I Love You?

Shorts
    Lovesick
    Abortive
    Not Not Not Not Not Enough Oxygen
    Schreber's Nervous Illness
    The Hospital at the Time of the Revolution
    The Judge's Wife
    The After-Dinner Joke
    Seagulls
    Three More Sleepless Nights

A Nick Hern Book

Escaped Alone first published in Great Britain as a paperback original in
2016 by Nick Hern Books Limited, The Glasshouse, 49a Goldhawk Road,
London W12 8QP, in association with the Royal Court Theatre, London

Reprinted 2017

Escaped Alone copyright © 2016 Caryl Churchill Limited

Caryl Churchill has asserted her right to be identified as the author of
this work

Front cover image: Root Design

Designed and typeset by Nick Hern Books
Printed in Great Britain by CPI Books (UK) Ltd

A CIP catalogue record for this book is available from the British Library

ISBN   978 1 84842 549 1

www.nickhernbooks.co.uk

facebook.com/nickhernbooks

twitter.com/nickhernbooks